JOHN GOLDING

FINDING THE ABSOLUTE

PIANO NOBILE

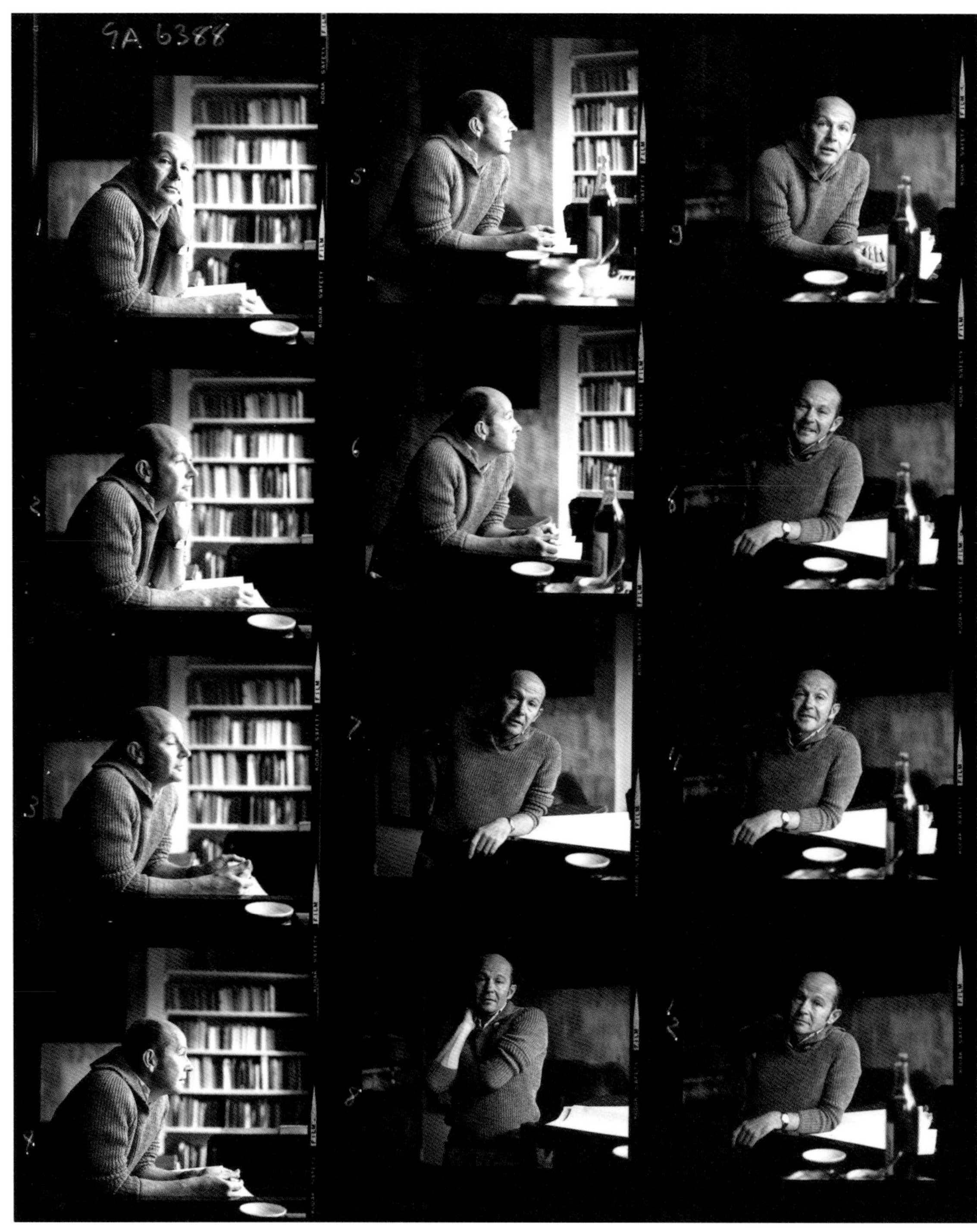

JOHN GOLDING

1929 - 2012

John Golding was born in Kent, England in 1929, but raised in Mexico. He attended the University of Toronto before returning to London to study for a Masters in History of Art and then a PhD at The Courtauld Institute of Art. His resulting thesis, written under Douglas Cooper and Anthony Blunt, formed the basis of his seminal book, *Cubism: A History and an Analysis, 1907-1914* (1959). Subsequently Golding became a much-loved teacher and academic at the Courtauld Institute, whilst simultaneously embarking upon a highly successful career as an artist. In 1981 Golding accepted the position of Senior Tutor in the painting department at the Royal College of Art, and he also held the Slade Professorship at Cambridge in 1978. He curated several landmark exhibitions including *Léger and Purist Paris* (1970) with Christopher Green, *Picasso: Painter/Sculptor* (1994) at the Tate and *Matisse/Picasso* (2002), which toured to the Tate, the Grand Palais in Paris and MoMA in New York.

As an artist, Golding had numerous one-man shows in prominent international galleries and museums, with his first solo show in London at Gallery One in 1962 and he also participated in many group exhibitions, including several international shows with his close friend, Op artist Bridget Riley. Golding was appointed a CBE in 1992 and elected a Fellow of the British Academy in 1994. His work is held in numerous prominent private and public collections including the Tate, the National Gallery of Scotland and MoMA. In 2000 his masterpiece on abstract art, *Paths to the Absolute*, was published, as a result of the A. W. Mellon Lectures in the Fine Arts series that he gave at Princeton in 1997. Spanning abstraction across continents and decades, this formalist account of the prominence of abstraction in modern art remains a hugely influential account of artists' search for the 'absolute' through abstraction. He died in April 2012.

Finding the Absolute

1 J. Golding, *Paths to the Absolute*, Princeton and London, 2000. p. 8.
2 Ibid.
3 Ibid., p.10.

In the preface to *Paths to the Absolute*, John Golding's last and highly influential book, the artist- art historian makes plain the difficulty in pursuing an abstract visual language: how many young artists who turn directly to abstraction do so to their peril - their 'artistic extinction' even, as they come to realise 'that they were not after all certain of what it was they were trying to say or express through the various idioms they had adopted.'[1] For the early abstractionists he considered, Mondrian, Malevich and Kandinsky, abstraction was a process arrived at through figurative practice. It is telling Golding wrote, that it was not until the end of the 1950s that artists felt they could turn directly to expression through solely abstract means. The central claim of *Paths to the Absolute* is that abstraction is 'heavily imbued with meaning'.[2] How to communicate meaning without pre-existing visual or narrative points of reference was Golding's life-long interest, whether as a scholar of Cubism or as a painter.

Golding argued eloquently that Cubism questioned 'the nature of perceived reality [and...] reinvented the language, the very syntax of painting and sculpture.'[3] In writing on Cubism, Golding also reinvented the language and methods of art history as a discipline, discussing it with an analytical focus and authority previously reserved for art prior to Modernism. As the most prescient advocate of abstract art, it is unsurprising that Golding's own artistic practice went hand in hand with his conceptualisation of art historical questions. To an extent, we can regard his painting as a means through which to explore art historical problems in another medium. This is not to say that one illustrates the other in any way, indeed Golding kept his two occupations separate. Few art historians today have a thorough knowledge of his painting, and fewer still have written about them.

Untitled
Oil and acrylic on board
35 x 25 cm / 13¾ x 9⅞ in

Golding started to produce abstract works in the mid 1960s, and from there on he continued to refine his visual language, moving away from offering descriptive titles. It is a development that mirrors the move from figuration to abstraction in the works of the early abstract artists he was to write on so eloquently. The works in this exhibition are significant as some of Golding's first explorations in abstraction, produced at a time when he started to paint more seriously. At first they appear bold and exuberant statements of great confidence, however they are characterised by subtlety, precision, and attention to detail that demands closer and longer looking. Layers of paint built up over time effect a depth and richness of complex colour; 'non-colours' of pale grey are full of blush, mauve or blue. Their textures aerate the canvas; and shapes superficially very similar turn out not to be identical, nor is their position (floating or grounded) the same between works. Looking at this group as a series we could evoke the metaphor of a visual theme and variation, where small changes stimulate different moods.

Adrian Stokes, writing in the catalogue for Golding's 1966 solo show at the Axiom Gallery, suggested the 'durability and progression' of these 'architectural' works. The show included paintings now displayed at Piano Nobile, *Niobe* (1966), *Gymnopédie* (1966), *Small Triptych*: *Red*, *Blue*, and *Yellow* (1966). Stokes emphasised the 'structure and variation one from another of a few motifs' which he believed were the articulation of 'stable moods or states of mind' in the same way that the mind informs the body.[4] Stokes' art criticism is marked for his prioritisation of sensational and bodily responses to works of art; however, Golding himself concurred with this interpretation. Indeed, reviewing Richard Wollheim's edited collection of Stokes' writing, *The Image in Form*, Golding remarked on Stokes' 'deeply intuitive approach' as a critic.[5] And speaking of his abstracts from 1970, Golding explained: 'I see them as objects to which the spectator, the human body or presence, can measure up to, or relate to.'

Scale was vitally important to Golding at this time. The exploration of formal relations in the *Triptych* of smaller works from 1966 is revisited in the monumental *Salome* (1966), and another work, similar in composition to *Salome*, *Phaestos – green* (1965-66) was shown at the 1967 Arts Council exhibition. Similarly, maquettes exploring material presence using cut-out and collage informed the larger works, fusing inspiration from American Abstract Expressionism with the traditions of Cubism. Look carefully at the contours of shapes and lines, and it is clear that layers of paint are built up in places, that Golding used tape to delineate areas, but also, contrary to cut-out, that shapes underwent a process of revision. Golding's technique was fundamentally hands on, materiality a key interest for its tactile quality. His use of floating pale blue rectangles mottled with flesh tones in *Narcissus* and *Gymnopédie*, however, emphasise materiality through their transparency: an impenetrable veil which could be lifted to reveal shapes beneath.

The Axiom Gallery was the home of hard-edged British abstractionists in the mid 1960s, inspired by the criticism of Clement Greenberg. Whilst Golding's abstracts brought together for this exhibition undoubtedly display the geometric and spatial interests of his contemporaries such as Sydney Nolan or Robyn Denny, it should be clear from the phenomenological interpretation offered by Stokes and Golding himself that Golding never adhered to Greenbergian Formalism either as a painter or an art historian . Rather these works can be thought of as a series, in which

4 A. Stokes, *John Golding Paintings, Charles Perry Sculpture*, Axiom Gallery Catalogue, 1966, p.6.

5 J. Golding, "The Eyes Have it", review of R. Wollheim (ed.) *The Image in Form: Selected Writings of Adrian Stokes*, *New York Review of Books*, 21st March 1974, pp. 38-39.

Narcissus, 1965
Oil and acrylic on canvas
142.2 x 188 cm / 56 x 74 in
Inscribed
"Narcissus Golding 65 56 x 74"
on reverse

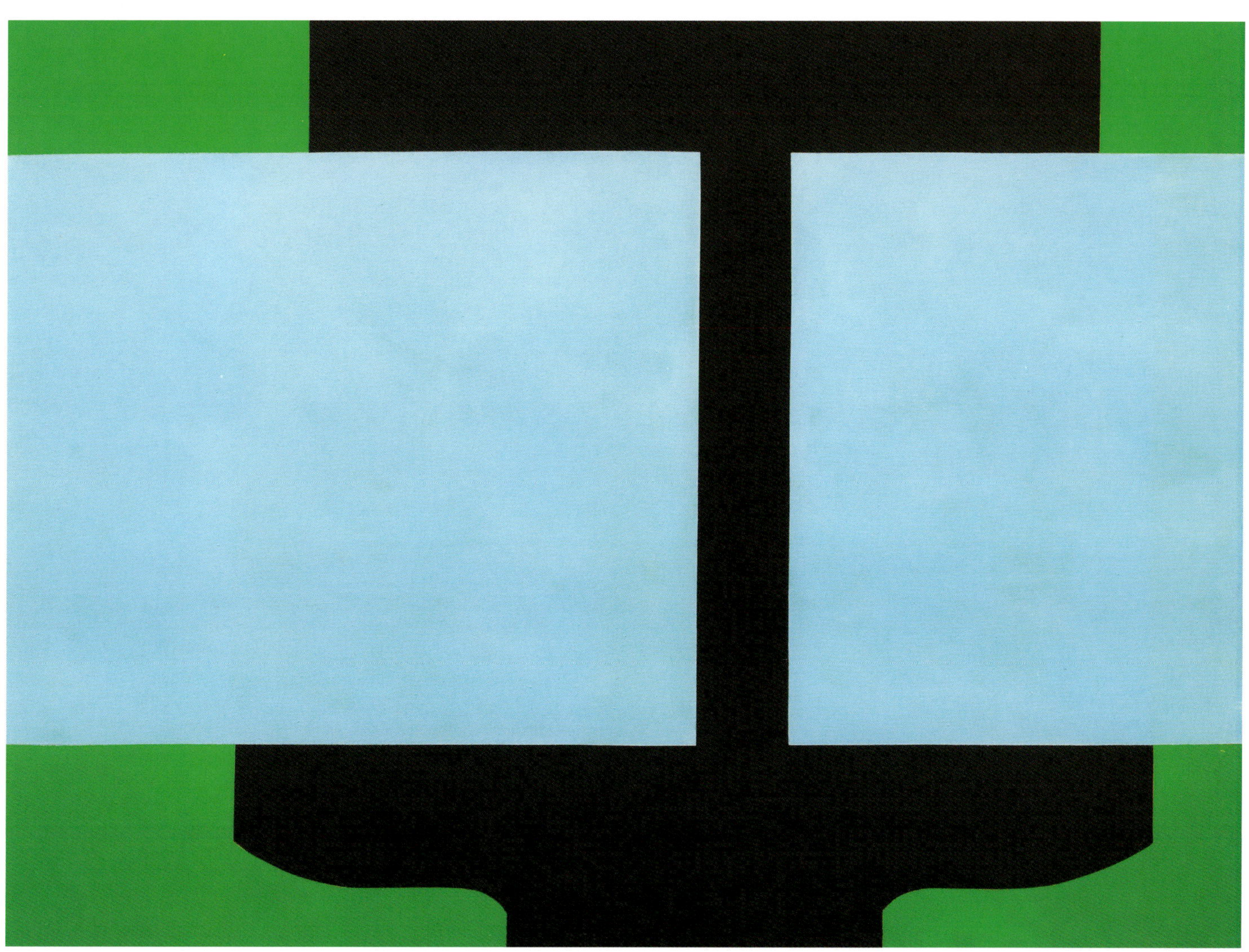

individual works reach out to each other and to the room in which they are situated in thoughtful dialogue. As Golding later commented, 'the pictures themselves become metaphors for bodies', objects therefore with which as viewers we are invited to establish a physical relation rather than merely a visual act of looking.[6] These canvases arrest the viewer with their presence, seducing us by scale, rich and vibrant colours, and bold shapes. In his ground-breaking essay "'Pop Art' since 1949", British art critic Lawrence Alloway noted the emergence of a second more abstract phase of pop which had a 'basis in common experience… without specifying its sources so legibly'.[7] Alloway cited artists such as Richard Smith, Robyn Denny and Patrick Caulfield as examples of the way in which pop sought to link abstract painting 'to the sensuous world of leisure.'[8] Golding's work was shown alongside these artists at the 1967 Arts Council exhibition of prominent contemporary practitioners, and it is evident that his choices of colour in the mid 1960s abstracts are redolent of this decade of experiment and revolution.

Golding's paintings from the 1960s are dynamic and youthful yet subtle and challenging; brimming with the influences of the past yet palpably created through the artistic language of the 1960s. Most of the paintings shown at Piano Nobile have not been seen for over forty years. Seeing these paintings together as a distinct and extraordinary phase of Golding's career offers a unique opportunity to appreciate Golding at the outset of his lifelong pursuit to realise the ever-elusive promise of the absolute through abstraction.

6 R. Wolheim, *John Golding*, New Haven, 1989, p. 9.
7 L. Alloway, "'Pop Art' since 1949" in R. Kalina (ed.), *Imagining the Present: Context, content and the role of the critic. Essays by Lawrence Alloway*, London and New York, 2006, p. 83.
8 Ibid., p. 84.

Vol de Nuit, 1966
Oil and acrylic on canvas
142 x 188 cm / 55⅞ x 74⅛ in
Inscribed
"Golding 66" on reverse

Piano Nobile Kings Place: Art and Music

Piano Nobile Kings Place is a new initiative which exhibits art that suggests a visual context to the music programme of Kings Place, in the belief that both arts may enrich one another through being experienced in close proximity. *Minimalism Unwrapped* is both a gift and a trial, for confusingly, Minimalist composers have collaborated with visual artists who art historians discuss in other contexts (e.g. Morton Feldman and Abstract Expressionism, John Cage and Neo-Dada). Indeed, in the Kings Place magazine, Steve Reich remembers the UK premiere of his *Drumming* (1971) at the Hayward Gallery's Rothko exhibition. If, however, we think of Minimalism in both media as meditation on essential qualities, we can see overlapping interests even where the artists involved would not refer to themselves as 'minimalist' – for example the 'maximalist' tendencies of Abstract Expressionism may find an interesting foil in the 'mystical' genre of Minimalist composition (Feldman, Arvo Pärt, John Tavener).

Gymnopédie, 1966
Oil and acrylic on canvas
165.1 x 228.6 cm / 65 x 90 in
Inscribed
"Golding '66 Gymnopedie
65 x 90" on reverse

John Golding's paintings from the mid 1960s focus on questions of form, scale and materiality, the artist– art historian's response to the materials of Cubism and monumentality of American Abstract Expressionism, Barnett Newman and Clyfford Still in particular. The works grouped in this exhibition may be considered as repetitions on a theme – note for example the way in which shapes recur in different colours and contexts across a number of works. On close examination, however, these are found not to be identical: such subtle differentiations orchestrate a rhythmic dynamism in composition. In theme then, they are not dissimilar from Minimalist composers' concern with the processes and languages of composing, their use of subtle variation in repeated motifs, micro-tonalities, and almost hypnotic evocations of time and space.

Golding's canvas entitled *Gymnopédie* is tantalising for its evocation of Erik Satie's piano compositions, but less is known about Golding's musical preferences than we might wish. It is true that Satie may be regarded as a precursor to Minimalism in his pairing down of musical language, and the title complements the abstract pleasingly, but it was Golding's partner James Joll who was the more musical of the two. Whatever we may conclude as regards specific examples, Golding's paintings share the excitement of innovation and exploration of the mid 1960s born of a shared historical context in which modes of expression were reinvented.

Dr Charlotte de Mille

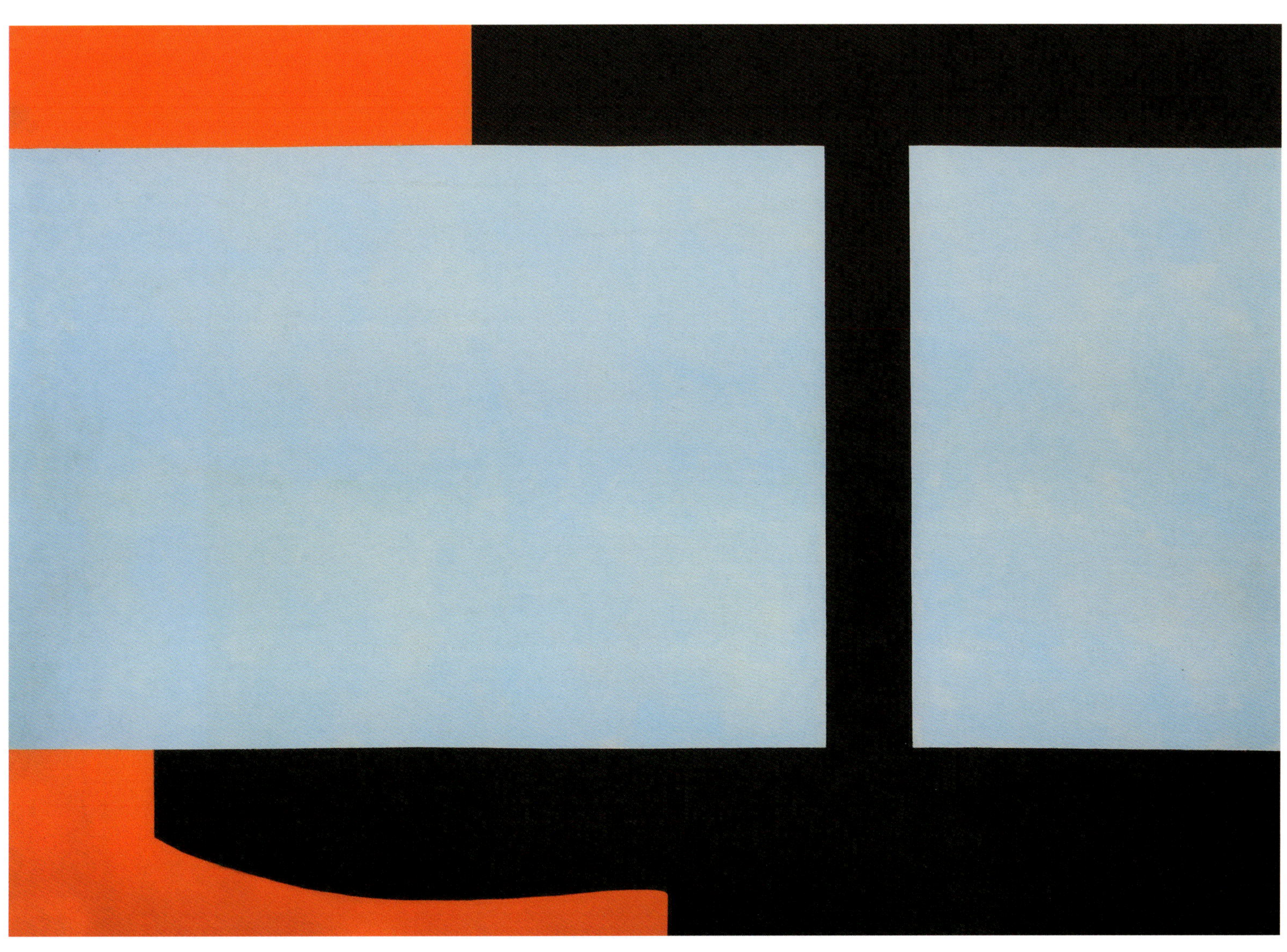

Untitled, c.1965
Oil and acrylic on canvas
142.2 x 188 cm / 56 x 74 in
Inscribed
"56 x 74" on reverse

following pages:

left
Portman Square, 1965-66
Acrylic and oil on canvas
165.1 x 162.1 cm / 65 x 65 in
Inscribed
"Golding Portman Square
65-66" on reverse

right
Square II, 1964
Acrylic and oil on canvas
165.1 x 162.1 cm / 65 x 65 in
Inscribed
"Golding 64 'Square II'" on reverse

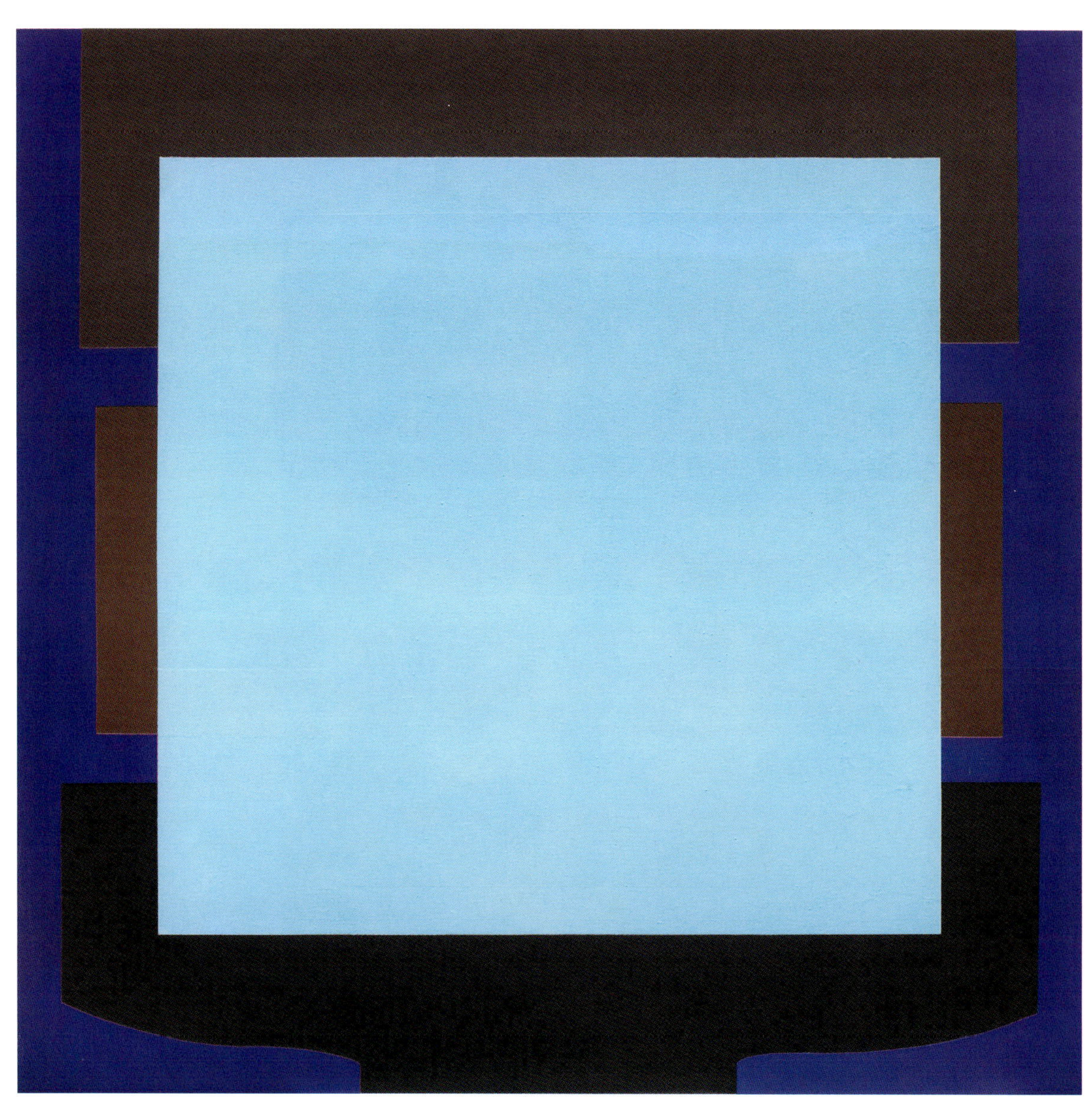

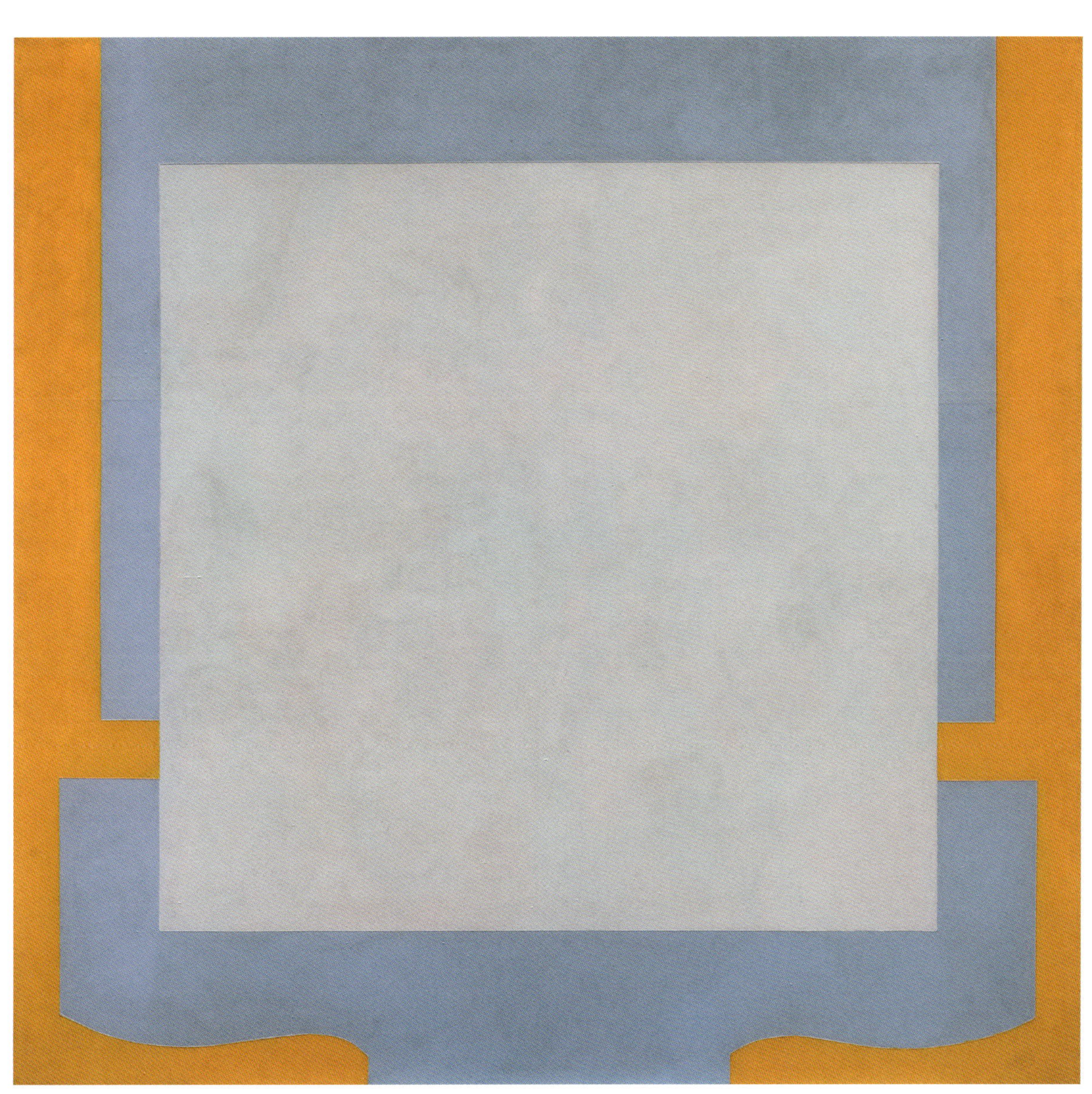

Niobe, 1966

Oil and acrylic on canvas
165 x 216 cm / 65 x 85⅛ in

Inscribed
"Golding - Niobe 66" on reverse

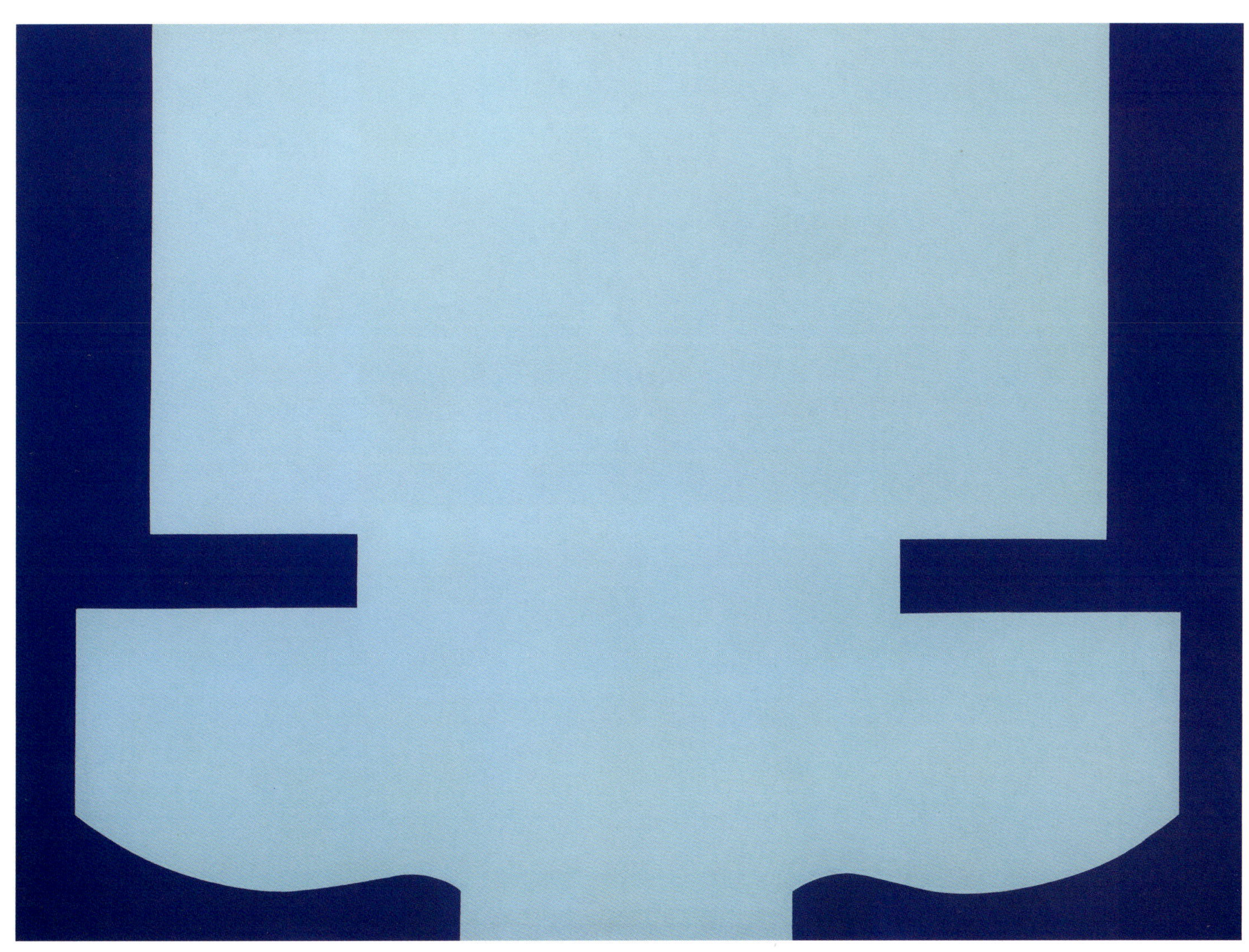

Small Triptych, 1966
Acrylic on board
Each panel:
61.3 x 45.7 cm / 24⅛ x 18 in

Signed and dated verso

Salome, 1966

Oil and acrylic on canvas
188 x 142 cm / 74⅛ x 55⅞ in

Inscribed
"Golding Salome Golding 66 74 x 56" on reverse

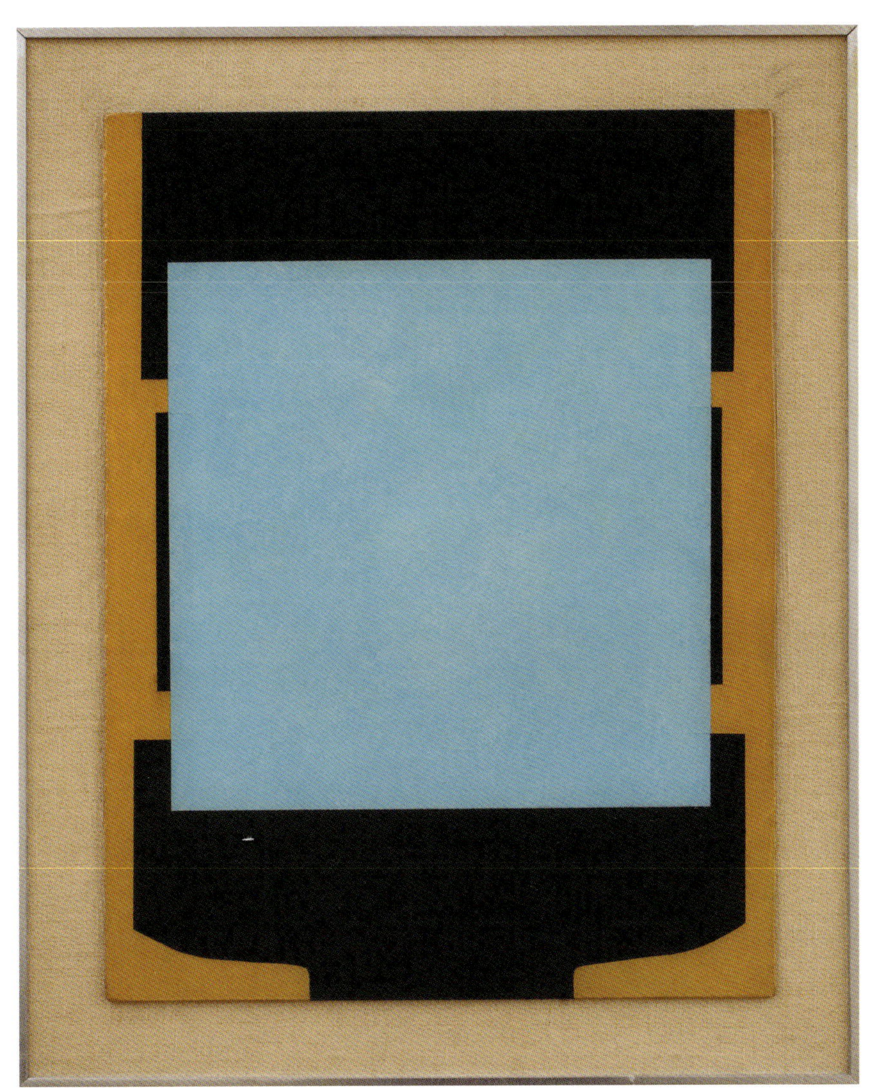
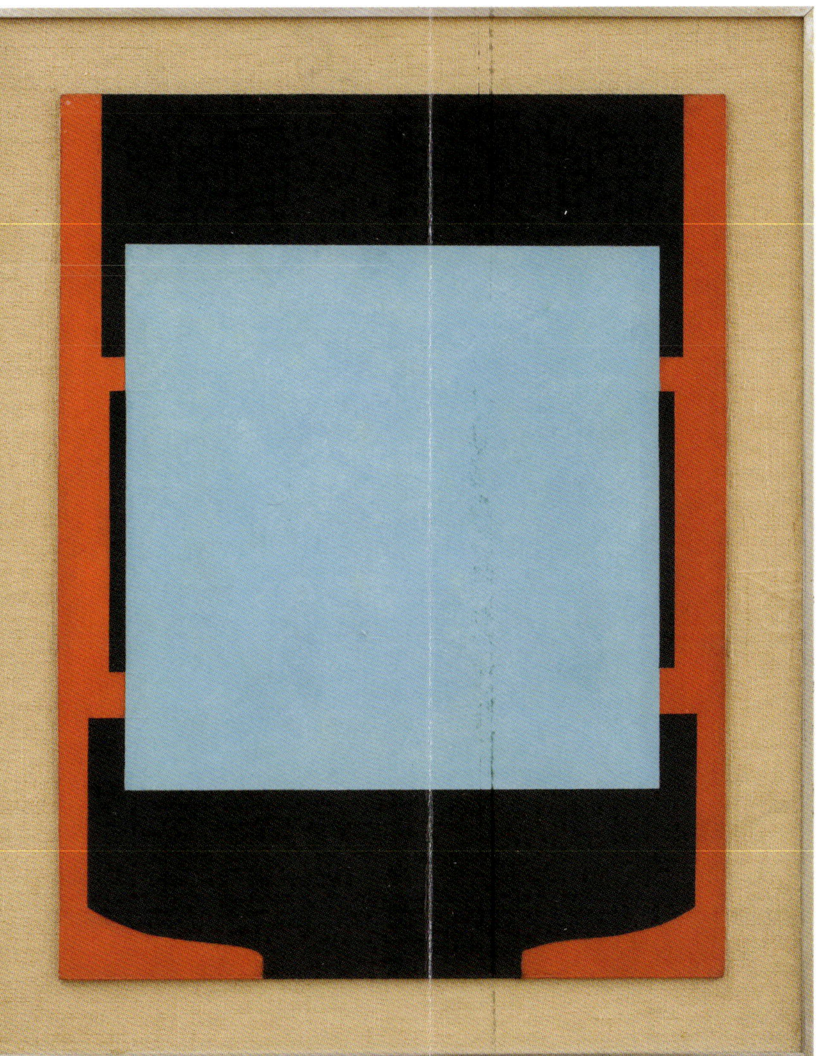
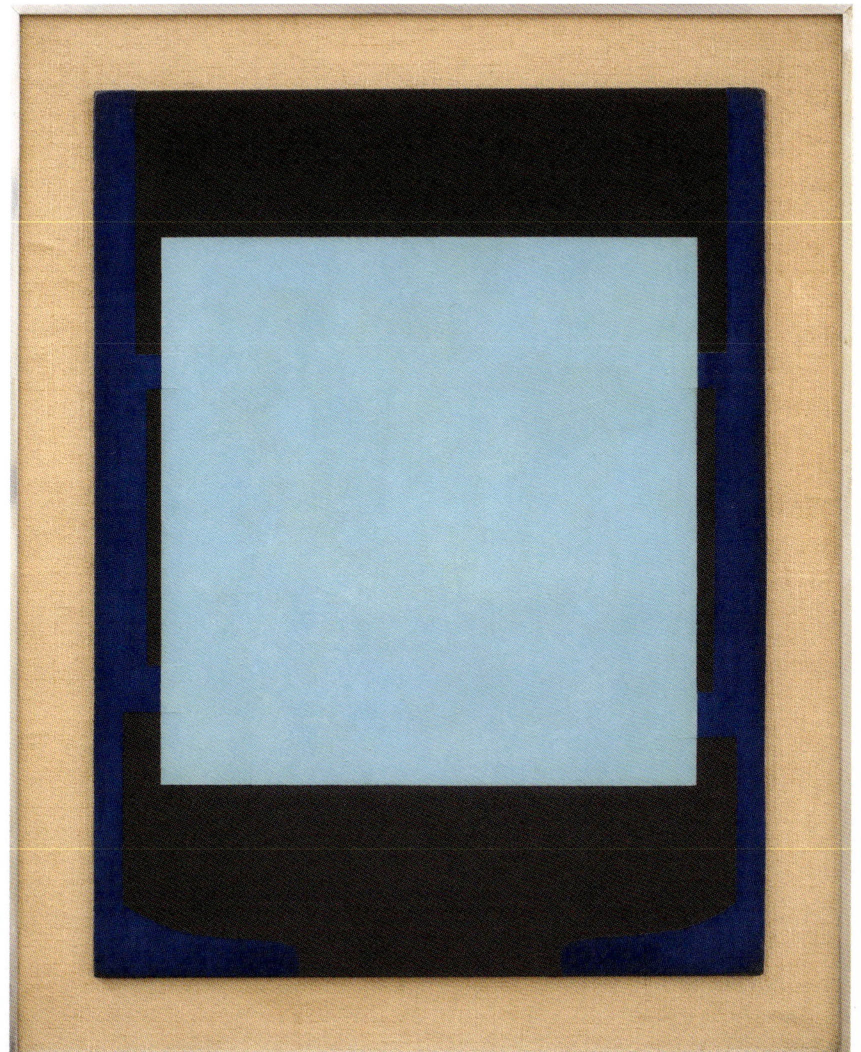

Salome, 1966
Oil and acrylic on canvas
188 x 142 cm / 74⅛ x 55⅞ in

Inscribed
"Golding Salome Golding 66 74 x 56" on reverse

Untitled, c.1967
Acrylic on canvas
229.9 x 165.1 cm / 90½ x 65 in

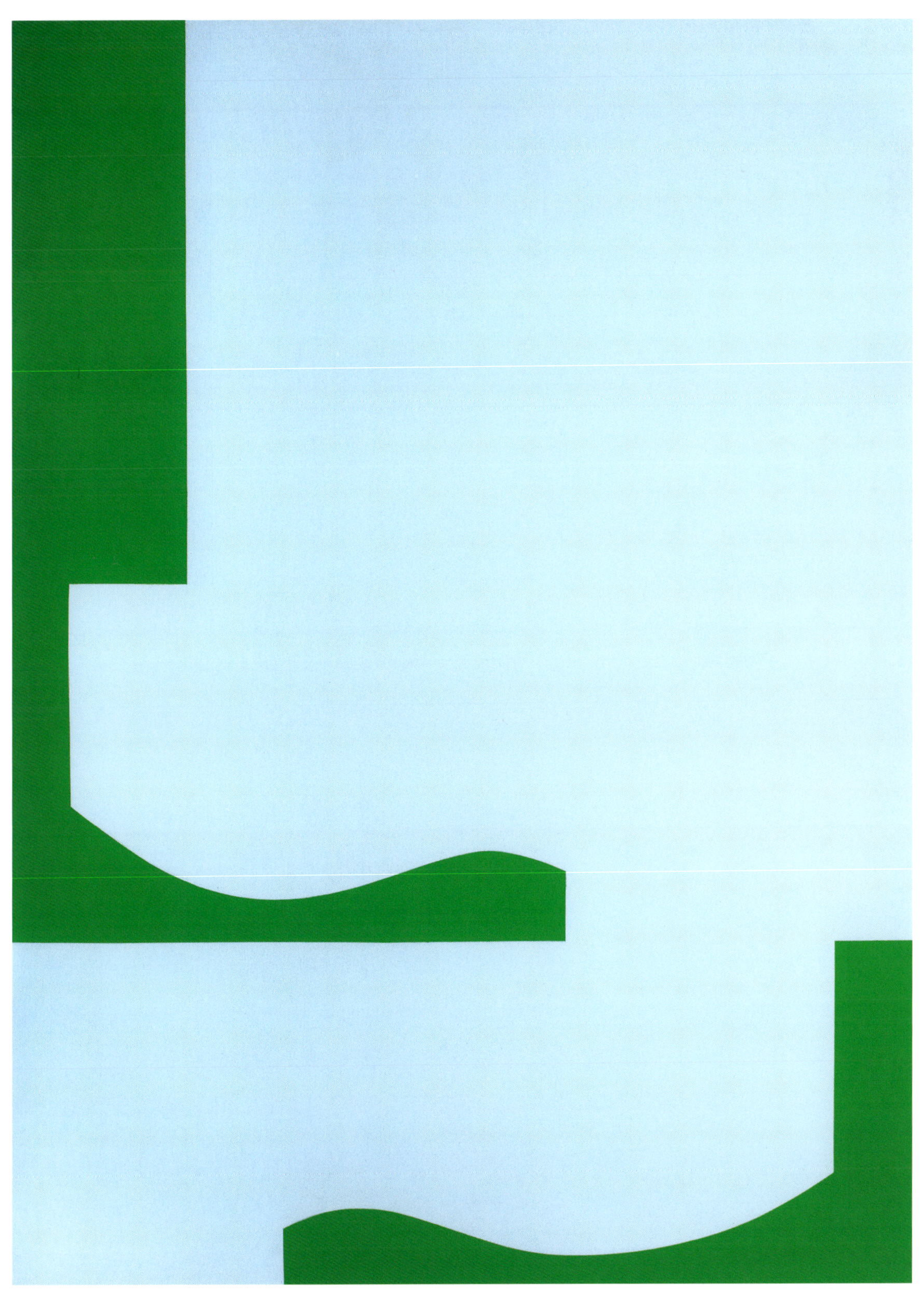

Predella (Red + Rose), 1967
Acrylic on canvas
230 x 165 cm / 90½ x 65 in

Inscribed
"Golding/Predella Painting/(Red + Rose)/'67" on reverse

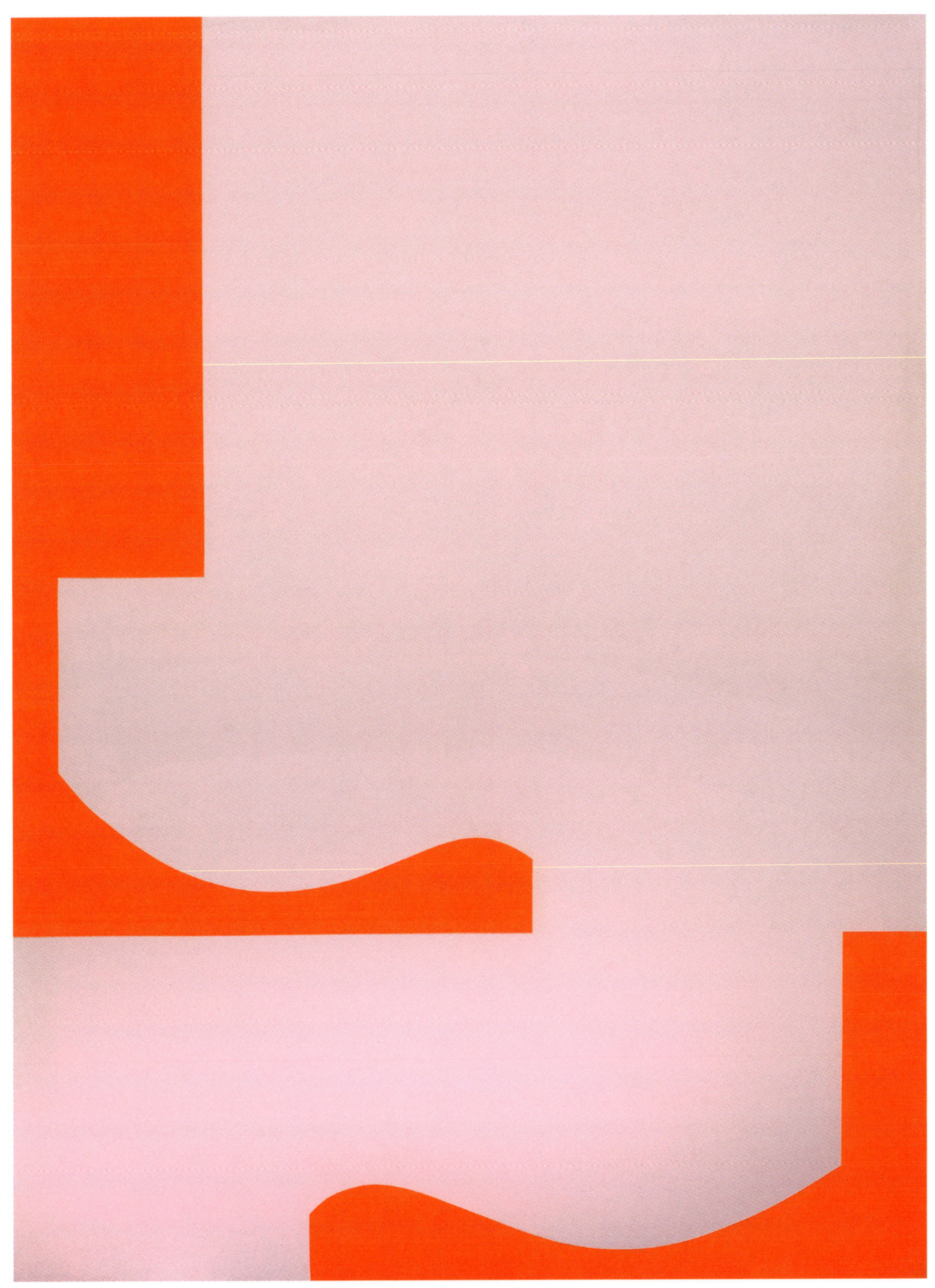

Blue Predella, 1967
Acrylic on canvas
228.6 x 165.1 cm / 90 x 65 in
Inscribed
"Blue Predella PTG 90 x 65 1967" on reverse

following pages:

left
Untitled 69, 1969
Acrylic on canvas
152.4 x 152.4 cm / 60 x 60 in
Inscribed
"Golding 69" on reverse

right
Untitled 69, 1969
Acrylic on canvas
152.4 x 152.4 cm / 60 x 60 in
Inscribed
"Golding 69" on reverse

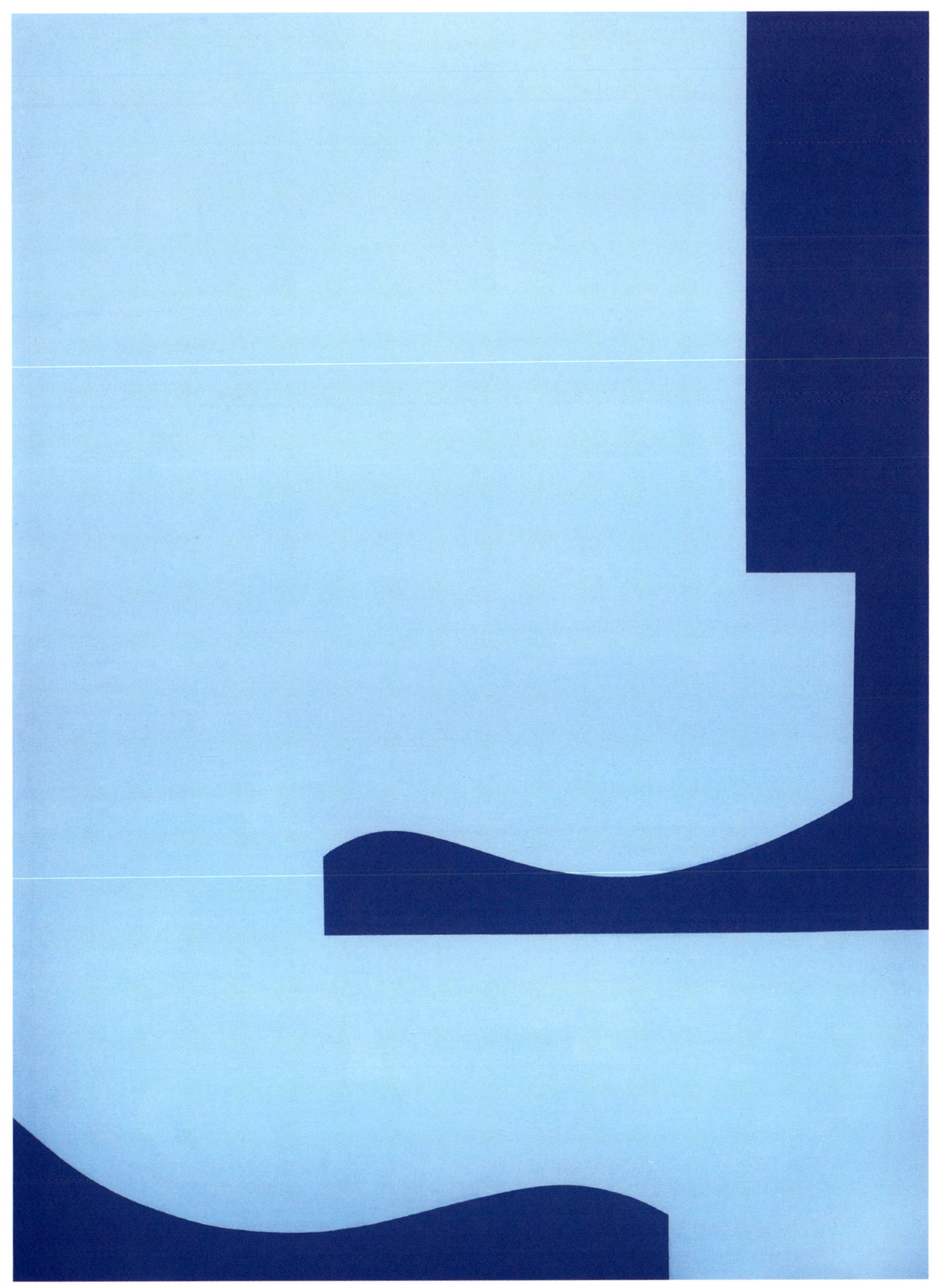

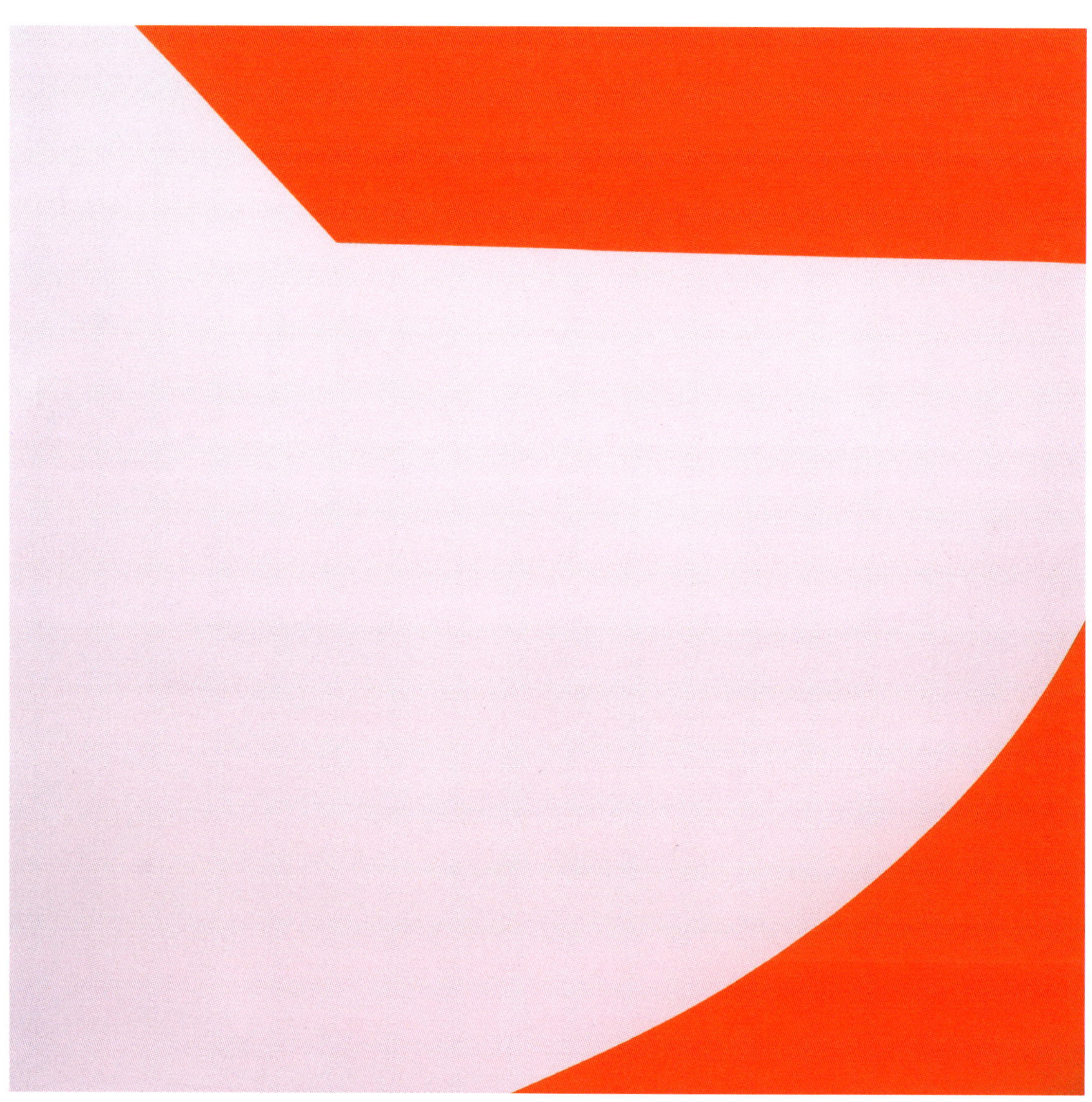

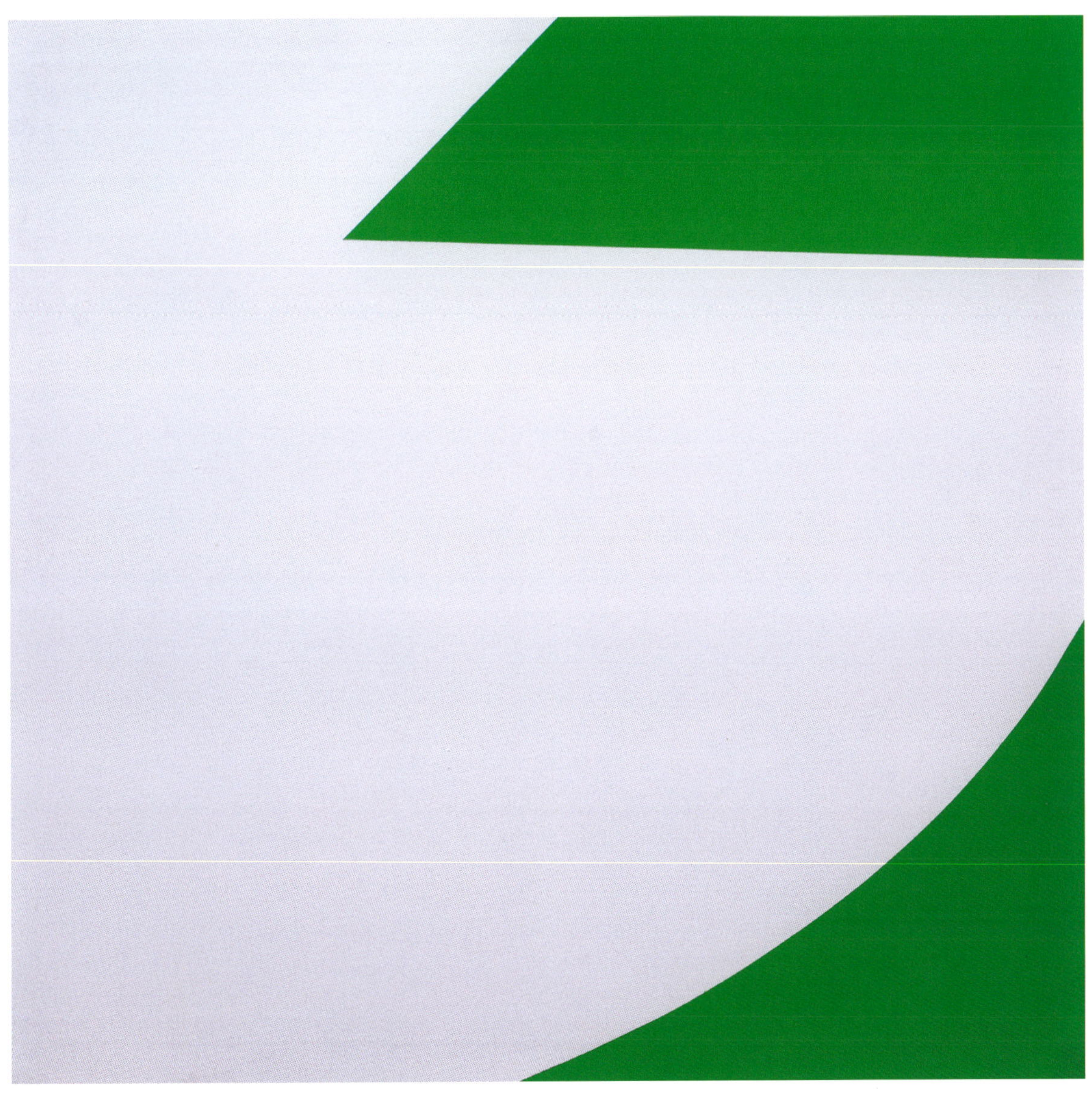

Chronology

1929 Born in Hastings
Educated in Mexico and Canada
1951-57 Postgraduate work at the Courtauld Institute of Art
1957 Obtained PhD for the Courtauld Institute of Art
1958 Solo exhibition at the Galeria Diana, Mexico City
1959 Cubism 1907-1914: A History and An Analysis is published, to wide acclaim
Began teaching at the Courtauld Institute of Art
1962 Solo exhibition at Gallery One, London
Group exhibition, Three Aspects of Contemporary Art at Whitworth Art Gallery, Manchester
1966 Group exhibition at the Axiom Gallery, Massachusetts
1970 Solo exhibition at Nigel Greenwood, London
Organised (with Christopher Green) Léger and Purist Paris exhibition at the Tate Gallery
1971 Solo exhibition at Museum of Modern Art, Oxford
1973 Marcel Duchamp: The Bride Stripped Bare by her Bachelors, Even is published as part of the important Art in Context series
1974 Group exhibition, British Painting '74 at Hayward Gallery, London
Lecture tour in Australia, coincided with solo exhibition at Holdsworth Gallery, Sydney
1975 Solo exhibition at Kettle's Yard, Cambridge
1977 Solo exhibition, John Golding: Recent Work at the National Gallery of Modern Art, Edinburgh
Solo exhibition John Golding: Paintings at Rowan Gallery, London
Group exhibition, British Painting 1952-77 at Royal Academy, London
Group exhibition, British Contemporary Art at Künstlerhaus Bregenz, Austria
1978-79 Appointed Slade Professor of Fine Art, University of Cambridge
1979 Solo exhibition at Rowan Gallery, London
1980 Solo exhibition at Riverside Studios, London
1981 Retired from the Courtauld Institute of Art
1982 Solo exhibition at Nishimura Gallery, Tokyo
1984 Solo exhibition at Coventry Gallery, Sydney
Solo exhibition, John Golding: Recent Paintings and Drawings at Juda Rowan Gallery, London
Group exhibition, Summer 1985 at Everard Read Gallery, Johannesburg, South Africa
Selected The Sculpture and Drawings of Henri Matisse, Hayward Gallery, London and Museum of Modern Art, New York
Trustee, Tate Gallery, London
1985 Solo exhibition at Nishimura Gallery, Tokyo
1988 Group exhibition, Works on Paper Selected by Marina Vaizey at Oxford Gallery, London
1989 Solo exhibition at Yale Center for British Art, Connecticut
Joint exhibition with Bridget Riley, HongKong Land, Hong Kong
1992 Appointed CBE
1994 Visions of the Modern, a collection of Golding's essays, is published
Curated Picasso: Painter/Sculptor exhibition at Tate Britain
Elected Fellow of the British Academy
2002 Paths to the Absolute: Mondrian, Malevich, Kandinsky, Pollock, Newman, Rothko and Still, published two years previously, is awarded the Mitchell Prize for the History of Art
2003 Solo exhibition at Roche Court, The New Art Centre, Salisbury
2010 Solo exhibition, John Golding at 80 at Tate Britain
2012 Died 9th of April in London
2012 Solo exhibition, Working Space: The 1971 paintings exhibited at the Museum of Modern Art, Oxford, at Annely Juda Fine Art, London
2015 Solo exhibition, John Golding: Finding the Absolute at Piano Nobile Kings Place, London
Exhibition at the Sainsbury Centre for Visual Arts, Abstraction and the Art of John Golding
Documentary film on John Golding by Bruno Wollheim with a working title of A Path to the Absolute

Selected Bibliography

1970 *Financial Times*, 3 November, Marina Vaizey
1971 *Sunday Times*, 17 October, John Russell
1972 *Guardian*, 12 January, Caroline Tisdall
1974 *Studio International*, June, "Principle, Appearance, Style," Alan Gouk
1974 *Art & Artists*, December, Toni del Renzio
1975 *Art International*, February, "A Note from John Golding," Elwyn Lynn
1975 *Arts Review*, 31 October, Eddie Wolfram
1975 *Times*, December, "Rich Contribution to Arts," John Vaizey
1975 *Tate Gallery Report, 1972-74*, "Acquisitions (Modern Collection)"
1975 Kettle's Yard Gallery exhibition leaflet: "John Golding: Paintings and Drawings," Marina Vaizey
1976 *Art International/The Art Spectrum*, January/February, "London Letter," Fenella Crichton
1976 *Arts Review*, 23 July, "Summer Show 2," Marina Vaizey
1977 *Observer*, 9 October, "Pure White and Flash Taste," William Feaver
1977 *Financial Times*, 22 October, "Abstract on Show," William Packer
1977 Scottish National Gallery of Modern Art, October, leaflet: "John Golding, Recent Work," Richard Calvorcoressi
1977 *Art Monthly*, November, "Two by Two They Went to the Ark," Charles Harrison and Victor Musgrave
1978 *Art in America*, March/April, "John Golding at Rowan," Suzi Gablik
1978 *Arts Review*, 26 May, "Rowan Artists," Guy Burns
1979 *Apollo*, October, "Round the Galleries," James Burr
1979 *Burlington Magazine*, November, "Current and Forthcoming Exhibitions," Richard Shone
1980 *Flash Art*, January/February, "London," Ian Bennett
1980 *Flash Art*, March/April, "Modern Painting and Modern Criticism in England," Ian Bennett
1980 *Arts Review*, May 23, "John Golding," Max Wykes-Joyce
1981 *Sunday Times*, 6 December, "The Art of the Alternative," Marina Vaizey
1984 "Pleated Light," Illustration in the Sunday Times, April 29, "Arts," Marina Vaizey
1984 *Pi* (University College London Students' Magazine), May 2, "Art Now," David Reiss
1988 *Sunday Times*, April 17, "Shaping Up to Abstracts," Marina Vaizey
1984 *Daily Telegraph*, April 19, "Speaking in Colours," Richard Dorment
1989 Yale Center for British Art exhibition publication: "John Golding," conversation with Richard Wollheim
1989 *New York Times*, 22 October, "Art; Abstractions by John Golding at Yale Center for British Art," Vivian Raynor
2001 *The Economist*, 12 January, "John Golding: Man of Colour"
2012 Annely Juda Fine Art exhibition catalogue: "John Golding: Working Space, the 1971 paintings exhibited at the Museum of Modern Art, Oxford," Edmund de Waal
2015 Piano Nobile exhibition catalogue: "John Golding: Finding the Absolute," Charlotte de Mille

Exhibition List of Works

Untitled
Oil and acrylic on board
35 x 25 cm / 13¾ x 9⅞ in

p.4

Narcissus, 1965
Oil and acrylic on canvas
142.2 x 188 cm / 56 x 74 in

Inscribed
"Narcissus Golding 65 56 x 74"
on reverse

p.7

Vol de Nuit, 1966
Oil and acrylic on canvas
142 x 188 cm / 55⅞ x 74⅛ in

Inscribed
"Golding 66" on reverse

p.9

Gymnopédie, 1966
Oil and acrylic on canvas
165.1 x 228.6 cm / 65 x 90 in

Inscribed
"Golding '66 Gymnopedie
65 x 90" on reverse

p.11

Untitled, c.1965
Oil and acrylic on canvas
142.2 x 188 cm / 56 x 74 in

Inscribed
"56 x 74" on reverse

p.13

Portman Square, 1965-66
Acrylic and oil on canvas
165.1 x 162.1 cm / 65 x 65 in

Inscribed
"Golding Portman Square
65-66" on reverse

p.14

Square II, 1964
Acrylic and oil on canvas
165.1 x 162.1 cm / 65 x 65 in

Inscribed
"Golding 64 'Square II'" on reverse

p.15

Niobe, 1966
Oil and acrylic on canvas
165 x 216 cm / 65 x 85⅛ in

Inscribed
"Golding - Niobe 66" on reverse

p.17

Small Triptych, 1966
Acrylic on board
Each panel:
61.3 x 45.7 cm / 24⅛ x 18 in

Signed and dated verso

pp.20-21

Salome, 1966
Oil and acrylic on canvas
188 x 142 cm / 74⅛ x 55⅞ in

Inscribed
"Golding Salome Golding 66 74 x 56"
on reverse

p.23

Untitled, c.1967
Acrylic on canvas
229.9 x 165.1 cm / 90½ x 65 in

p.25

Predella (Red + Rose), 1967
Acrylic on canvas
230 x 165 cm / 90½ x 65 in

Inscribed
"Golding/Predella Painting/
(Red + Rose)/'67" on reverse

p.27

Blue Predella, 1967
Acrylic on canvas
228.6 x 165.1 cm / 90 x 65 in

Inscribed
"Blue Predella PTG 90 x 65 1967"
on reverse

p.29

Untitled 69, 1969
Acrylic on canvas
152.4 x 152.4 cm / 60 x 60 in

Inscribed
"Golding 69" on reverse

p.30

Untitled 69, 1969
Acrylic on canvas
152.4 x 152.4 cm / 60 x 60 in

Inscribed
"Golding 69" on reverse

p.31